BLUEPRINTS OF DESTINY

THE REVELATION IN GOD'S SILENCE

Author

DR. NEVILLE G. WOLLISTON

CONTENT

Introduction

1 CAN YOU TRUST HIM 2

2 HE HAS YOUR BEST INTEREST AT HEART 16

3 HE IS CAPABLE 26

4 HIS INTEGRITY 39

5 HIS PLANS FOR YOU 54

<u>Introduction</u>

There are divine plans in motion, plans for our lives that we are often unaware of. As we deepen our relationship with God and allow the Holy Spirit to dwell within us, we will better understand these plans, and can become active in bringing them to fruition. Our faith becomes stronger when we embrace that we are an integral part of God's plan, and God's plans are amazing.

"Blueprints of Destiny: The Revelation in God's Silence" is a book that aims to show you how, even in the moments of God's silence, His intricate plans are unfolding for you, your family, and the world. Moreover, some of us possess the gift of prophetic symbolism, meaning through the events of our lives, God is communicating His plans for the world. All of God's children have a prophetic nature, which allows them to see and hear things from the spiritual realm prior to the manifestations in the physical world.

The Book of Revelation details the destruction that will come to the earth, much of which is unfolding now. For us to thrive during these times, we must be sealed in God, living as one with the Holy Spirit. We have a significant role in God's restoration of humanity, and now is the time for us to fully comprehend how God communicates, embrace the call of God upon our lives, and have confidence in His plans, even when He is silent.

Chapter One

CAN YOU TRUST HIM

This day was just like any other, my vacation in Dubai was coming to an end. Whether fortunate or not, it was time to say goodbye to a place that, in my opinion, is unmatched in its luxury and exclusivity. My journey back to the United States included a layover in Zurich, Switzerland, before continuing to New York. We arrived at the airport early, went through the required security checks and headed to our gate of departure, knowing how crucial it was for us not to miss our flight. Since we had plenty of time before boarding, we decided to relax in the business lounge.

The flight from Dubai to Zurich was to last about seven hours, which was not too bad. We boarded the plane on time and the flight attendants were very helpful in explaining the safety procedures. Being a seasoned traveler, I did not expect anything unusual to happen that day. The plane smoothly taxied down the runway and took off within minutes. When we reached an altitude of around thirty thousand feet, the pilot came on the intercom and gave us the flying time and the weather conditions in Zurich. He told us to sit back, relax, and enjoy the flight, something I have heard many times before.

During the flight, the experience was generally uninterrupted, except for a few minor disturbances. Despite my personal preference against sleeping during flights, I managed to catch some rest intermittently. Since the flight was set to arrive in Zurich the following morning, breakfast was to be served before landing.

Approximately ninety minutes prior to landing, the passengers were served breakfast. After the meal, the pilot made an announcement, informing us that our destination was near. He provided a weather report and expressed gratitude for our decision to fly with the airline, hoping to welcome us again on a future flight. The passengers, including myself, were full of excitement. It would only be another twenty to twenty-five minutes before we touched down. It was my first-time visiting Switzerland, I was filled with anticipation. The seat belt sign eventually illuminated, and the pilot instructed everyone to prepare for landing. However, approximately fifteen minutes before landing, the aircraft began to shake. I initially assumed it was not a cause for concern, I was completely wrong. The aircraft began to shake intensely, and the vibration grew increasingly severe. At one point, it felt as though the plane was rapidly accelerating and then decelerating. As the shaking persisted, I could not help but wonder what was happening. This was not typical turbulence, as the motion was not limited to up-and-down movements, but included side-to-side and back-and-forth motions.

To say that I was concerned would be an understatement. Although I have experienced turbulence before, this was unlike anything I had ever encountered. Other passengers were similarly affected, with some visibly shaken and expressing their fear through shouts or gasps.

During the turbulence the pilot remained silent, causing further distress to the passengers. It is customary for pilots to communicate with passengers during such situations to provide reassurance and alleviate anxiety. However, no such communication was made, leaving the passengers to cope with their fears. Attempting to remain composed, I felt overwhelmed by the situation and repeatedly stated, "It is not supposed to end like this." I kept saying those words and reassuring myself, "it is not supposed to end like this." The proximity to the ground, with houses and cars visible outside the window, added to the concern. Despite the visible surroundings, there was no sign of the runway, leaving the passengers to wonder if they would make it or crash into the houses below.

After an extended period of apprehension, the pilot skillfully landed the aircraft without any issues. This was met with a collective sigh of relief from all of us on board. As we disembarked, the air hostess welcomed us to Zurich and expressed her hope that we had enjoyed the flight. We were all taken back by this statement, as we had just experienced a harrowing ordeal. Though we were grateful to have survived, the intensity of the experience left us reeling for several minutes.

Upon arrival and subsequent retrieval of our luggage to clear customs, I perceived what I believed to be the voice of God, albeit internally. The words that resonated within me were forceful and thought-provoking:

"What do you do when God is silent?"

Upon hearing these words, I immediately began to engage in self-examination and repentance. The question of "*What do you do when God is silent*" is a crucial one. It is similar to being on a plane with a pilot who remains silent during a harrowing experience. Can we trust that the pilot will bring us to our destination safely? Similarly, during times of turmoil and hardship, when God remains silent, can we trust Him? These questions inspired me to write this book. While initially I considered preaching on the topic, I felt an overwhelming urge to compose this text instead. My hope is that it will prove beneficial to those experiencing challenges in life.

"What do you do when God is silent?"

Upon the utterance of those words resonating within my spirit, my thoughts shifted to the biblical character Job, whom God held in high regard. The more we anchor ourselves in prayer, listening to God and obeying His instructions immediately, more of the plans for our lives are revealed, even when God seems silent.

"There was a man in the land of Uz, whose name was Job; and that man was perfect and upright, and one that feared God, and eschewed evil." Job 1:1

God took such delight in Job that He engaged in a contest with Satan. In Chapter 1, verse 8 of the book of Job, the Lord spoke to Satan and asked if he had considered his servant Job, who was a perfect and upright man, one who feared God, and avoided evil. However, this was only the beginning of a series of events that would challenge and change Job's life. Despite God's trust and delight in Job, Job found himself in an unexpected and unanticipated situation. What does one do when they are certain that God is with them and has their back, yet finds themselves in an unforeseen circumstance? In times of distress, one may find themselves in an unfavorable situation, much like Job. To compound the issue, it can feel as though God is silent. This begs the question, *"What do you do when God is silent?"* When seeking guidance, but hearing no words; when seeking assurance, but finding none; when seeking comfort, but finding no solace. What actions should be taken in such circumstances?

Job Chapter 10 verses 1 through 22 we read what appears to be Job's complaint:

My soul is weary of my life; I will leave my complaint upon myself; I will speak in the bitterness of my soul. I will say unto God, do not condemn me; shew me wherefore thou contend with me. Is it good unto thee that thou shouldest oppress, that thou shouldest despise the work of thine hands, and shine upon the counsel of the wicked?

Hast thou eyes of flesh? Or seest thou as man seeth? Are thy days as the days of man? Are thy years as man's days, that thou enquire after

mine iniquity, and search after my sin? Thou knowest that I am not wicked; and there is none that can deliver out of thine hand. Thine hands have made me and fashioned me together round about; yet thou dost destroy me. Remember, I beseech thee, that thou hast made me as the clay; and wilt thou bring me into dust again?

Hast thou not poured me out as milk, and curdled me like cheese? Thou hast clothed me with skin and flesh, and hast fenced me with bones and sinews. Thou hast granted me life and favour, and thy visitation hath preserved my spirit. And these things hast thou hid in thine heart: I know that this is with thee.

If I sin, then thou markest me, and thou wilt not acquit me from mine iniquity. If I be wicked, woe unto me; and if I be righteous, yet will I not lift up my head. I am full of confusion; therefore, see thou mine affliction; For it increaseth. Thou huntest me as a fierce lion: and again thou shewest thyself marvellous upon me.

Thou renewest thy witnesses against me, and increasest thine indignation upon me; changes and war are against me. Wherefore then hast thou brought me forth out of the womb? Oh, that I had given up the ghost, and no eye had seen me!

I should have been as though I had not been; I should have been carried from the womb to the grave. Are not my days few? cease then, and let me alone, that I may take comfort a little, Before I go whence I shall not return, even to the land of darkness and the shadow of death; A land of darkness, as darkness itself; and of the shadow of death, without any order, and where the light is as darkness.

In this chapter, Job articulates his claim and complaint, yet despite this, God remains silent. It takes until chapter 38 for God to finally respond.

What should one do when God takes a long time to respond, or doesn't respond at all?

For Job, it must have been an extremely nerve-racking experience. He couldn't comprehend why his life had suddenly turned upside down. It took 28 whole chapters for God to utter a single word. What should we do when God takes His time, like in the case of Lazarus, or when He is completely silent? Can we still trust Him? Let me assure you that even when God is silent, He is still speaking. We must learn to discern the silence of our Father and never mistake it for incompetence. In **Chapter 38, when God finally speaks**, He challenges Job with a series of difficult questions.

Then the Lord answered Job out of the whirlwind, and said, Who is this that darkeneth counsel by words without knowledge? Gird up now thy loins like a man; for I will demand of thee, and answer thou me. Where wast thou when I laid the foundations of the earth? declare, if thou hast understanding. Who hath laid the measures thereof, if thou knowest? Or who hath stretched the line upon it?

Whereupon are the foundations thereof fastened? Or who laid the corner stone thereof; When the morning stars sang together, and all the sons of God shouted for joy? Or who shut up the sea with doors, when it brakes forth, as if it had issued out of the womb?

When I made the cloud the garment thereof, and thick darkness a swaddling band for it, and brake up for it my decreed place, and set bars and doors, and said, Hitherto shalt thou come, but no further: and here shall thy proud waves be stayed?

Hast thou commanded the morning since thy days; and caused the dayspring to know his place; That it might take hold of the ends of the earth, that the wicked might be shaken out of it? It is turned as clay to the seal; and they stand as a garment. And from the wicked their light is withholden, and the high arm shall be broken.

Hast thou entered into the springs of the sea? or hast thou walked in the search of the depth?

Have the gates of death been opened unto thee? or hast thou seen the doors of the shadow of death?

Hast thou perceived the breadth of the earth? declare if thou knowest it all.

Where is the way where light dwelleth? and as for darkness, where is the place thereof, that thou shouldest take it to the bound thereof, and that thou shouldest know the paths to the house thereof? Knowest thou it, because thou wast then born? or because the number of thy days is great?

Hast thou entered into the treasures of the snow? or hast thou seen the treasures of the hail, which I have reserved against the time of trouble, against the day of battle and war?

By what way is the light parted, which scattereth the east wind upon the earth? Who hath divided a watercourse for the overflowing of waters, or a way for the lightning of thunder;

To cause it to rain on the earth, where no man is; on the wilderness, wherein there is no man; To satisfy the desolate and waste ground; and to cause the bud of the tender herb to spring forth? Hath the rain a father? or who hath begotten the drops of dew?

Out of whose womb came the ice? and the hoary frost of heaven, who hath gendered it? The waters are hid as with a stone, and the face of the deep is frozen.

Canst thou bind the sweet influences of Pleiades, or loose the bands of Orion?

Canst thou bring forth Mazzaroth in his season? or canst thou guide Arcturus with his sons?

Knowest thou the ordinances of heaven? canst thou set the dominion thereof in the earth? Canst thou lift up thy voice to the clouds, that abundance of waters may cover thee?

Canst thou send lightnings, that they may go and say unto thee, here we are? Who hath put wisdom in the inward parts? Or who hath given understanding to the heart? Who can number the clouds in wisdom?

Or who can stay the bottles of heaven, when the dust groweth into hardness, and the clods cleave fast together? Wilt thou hunt the prey for the lion? or fill the appetite of the young lions, when they couch in their dens, and abide in the covert to lie in wait? Who provideth for the raven his food? When his young ones cry unto God, they wander for lack of meat.

I would like to offer you assurance today, irrespective of your present circumstances. Even if it appears as though God is not communicating with you, let me remind you that His silence does not mean He is not speaking. The crucial question is, can you place your trust in Him even when He is not uttering a single word?

Chapter Two

HE HAS YOUR BEST INTEREST AT HEART

The unfortunate and very unpleasant encounter left a lasting impression on me. It was an experience that compelled me to ask some difficult questions and it put my faith to the test. My belief in the aviation sector, the airline we traveled with, and particularly the pilot responsible for our secure landing, were challenged. Amidst the turbulence, I had to reassure myself that the pilot had our safety as the top priority. In the midst of the intense shaking, I had to reassure myself that he, the pilot, had our best interest at heart.

The pilot had a significant responsibility of ensuring the safety of over four hundred passengers and crew members on board, in addition to looking after his own well-being to return home to his family. Reflecting upon this, it occurred to me how similar this is to the role of God, our Heavenly Father, who always has our best interests at heart, regardless of the challenges we face or the circumstances we find ourselves in.

One of my favorite biblical verses, *Jeremiah 29:11*, affirms this belief*, "I know the thoughts that I think towards you saith the Lord thoughts of peace and not of evil to give you an expected end."*

Jeremiah 29:11 is the scripture verse that my Mother would frequently remind me of, particularly during times of hardship and difficulty. Currently, I am resolutely convinced that **our Heavenly Father always acts in our best interests**, without any doubt whatsoever. Despite the fact that life can present challenges that are difficult to comprehend, much like the ones experienced by Job, we must remain steadfast in our faith.

We are reminded by scripture in *John 10:10,* *"The thief cometh not, but for to kill steal and destroy, I am come that they may have life and that they may have it more abundantly."*

It is undeniable that we must hold the belief that *the God of the universe has our best interests in mind.* This is evidenced by the fact that He created us in His own image, suggesting that He has great plans for our lives. It is my conviction that you and I are here because God has a specific purpose for us, and that the world needs us. Each person has been born with a unique purpose to fulfill in God's grand scheme.

The absence of Martin Luther King Jr., Nelson Mandela, and Rosa Parks in our world would be inconceivable. Moreover, can you fathom a world without your own presence, or the absence of your home, family, and community? Although we may not be Rosa Parks or Nelson Mandela, it is certain that each of us has a unique opportunity to make a positive impact in some capacity.

It is important to bear in mind that remarkable feats were accomplished by ordinary individuals. Harriet Tubman, for instance, established and managed the Underground Railroad. George Washington Carver is another example of an ordinary person who invented peanut butter, along with Garret Morgan who invented the stop light. We must exercise caution and not allow societal expectations, cultural norms, or environmental factors to dictate our potential.

Frequently, we become confined to the labels that others have imposed on us, instead of embracing our true identity as defined by God.

During his time on earth, Jesus was resolute in making it clear that he was here to carry out the will of his Father. This conviction was evident even at the tender age of twelve, when he declared his purpose to his parents who were searching for him. As children of the Almighty, it is imperative that we constantly remind ourselves that we too are here on purpose, and *that God has our best interests at heart*. It is essential that we adopt this mindset, knowing our identity and our source. The pilot's ultimate responsibility was not only to expertly take off the aircraft, but more importantly, to ensure that we reach our intended destination.

In order to achieve success, we must have the right mindset and approach to life. This includes understanding our identity and purpose. The role of a pilot extends beyond simply getting an aircraft off the ground, although this is certainly a skill that requires expertise. Ultimately, the pilot's primary responsibility is to ensure that passengers arrive at their intended destination safely. While there may have been challenges that the pilot faced while navigating this large aircraft through the skies, these difficulties may not have been apparent to us as passengers. It is likely that the pilot's focus was not to cause alarm, but rather to remain vigilant and committed to completing the mission at hand.

If we are not careful, there are times when the Devil can cause us to lose our focus, just as he did with Peter while he was walking towards Christ on the water. Like most of us, Peter was doing well until he lost his focus and took his eyes off the great I AM. Let it never be said of us that we have lost our focus. We need to remain focused on our goals, and on the fact that *the God of the universe has our best interests at heart*. This reminds me of a tragedy that occurred in our country many years ago, specifically in 1972. It was a dark December night when a Lockheed jumbo jet crashed into the Florida Everglades, resulting in the loss of 101 lives. This terrible accident remains one of the deadliest crashes in the history of the United States.

An intriguing aspect of this incident is that the aircraft's essential components and systems were operating without any issues. The airplane had the capacity to land safely at its intended destination, Miami, which was merely 20 miles (32km) away.

However, during the final approach, the crew observed that a particular green light had not illuminated. The light served to indicate if the nose landing gear had extended adequately. As a result, the pilots decided to abort the approach, entered a circling holding pattern above the pitch-black Everglades, and focused on investigating the problem.

Their focus on the issue was so intense that they failed to notice that the plane was gradually descending towards the dark swamp below. By the time someone noticed the impending disaster, it was too late to prevent it. As a result, 101 people lost their lives.

Following the plane crash, investigators conducted an inquiry to determine the cause of the accident. The investigation revealed that everything was functioning correctly, except for a single burned-out light bulb. This small component, which was only worth 20 cents, triggered a chain of events that led to the tragic death of over 100 people.

It is important to note that the malfunctioning light bulb was not the direct cause of the accident. Instead, the crew became sidetracked, focusing on something that seemed important at the moment, while losing sight of what truly mattered. This scenario highlights the significance of staying focused on the most pivotal things. It is not only pilots who are at risk of losing sight of what matters most; everyone is vulnerable to this tendency. For instance, a driver who concentrates on the road has a much higher chance of reaching their destination without any accidents than someone who is focused on sending text messages on their phone.

As human beings, we must understand what is most important in life. The Light of Christ teaches us this.

As followers of Christ, we have the indwelling of the Holy Spirit, who serves as our "constant companion" and guides us in matters of eternal significance. It is worth restating, ***"the Lord has our best interest at heart."***

This is a song we used to sing in the old church:

"VICTORY, VICTORY SHALL BE MINE
VICTORY, VICTORY SHALL BE MINE
IF I HOLD MY PEACE
LET THE LORD FIGHT MY BATTLES
VICTORY, VICTORY SHALL BE MINE"
Reverend James Cleveland

These words emphasize the importance of allowing the Lord to fight our battles. While most individuals are capable of delivering an exceptional speech or essay on the topic of "what matters most," our downfall lies in failing to align our actions with our conscience.

Take a moment to pause and reflect on where your heart and thoughts currently reside. Are you prioritizing the things that truly matter? Your habits during moments of solitude can provide valuable insight. When deadlines and external pressures are absent, do your thoughts focus on fleeting, temporary matters, or do they center on things of eternal significance?

During the aircraft's descent, we encountered a severe shaking that was beyond our control. Despite this, the pilot remained focused on the task at hand - bringing the aircraft safely to land.

As individuals, we must identify the factors that impede our progress and hinder us from fulfilling the call of God on our lives. These hindrances may not necessarily be negative; in fact, they may provide temporary satisfaction. However, it is important to exercise caution and avoid going overboard, as excessive indulgence in even the good things can be detrimental. For instance, a gardener could spend all his time pulling weeds from the soil (the physical) and neglect the weeds that pose a threat to his soul (the spiritual).

We must maintain a balanced life, even with regards to Church-related activities. Overindulging in programs can potentially distract us and consume our time, diverting our attention from the more important matters. As individuals who profess our love for our Heavenly Father and His children, we must exhibit this love through purposeful actions that prioritize matters of eternal value.

Chapter Three

HE IS CAPABLE

It is uncommon for individuals to board an airplane and immediately request to see the pilot's credentials. Similarly, one would not enter an emergency room and ask for proof of medical staff qualifications. Such a request would be considered impolite, offensive, and unprofessional. We rely on the expertise of professionals in our daily lives, particularly those who possess skills outside of our own areas of expertise. While enduring the stressful flight, I reminded myself that the pilot was not only qualified, but also capable of executing a safe landing. According to Webster's dictionary, "capable" refers to possessing the necessary ability, fitness, or quality required to accomplish a specific task. I realized that the pilot was indeed capable of successfully navigating us through this challenging situation. After considering the extensive training that the pilot must have undergone during fight school, coupled with his previous experience flying this type of aircraft, there seemed to be no reason for concern. Although the intense shaking of the plane persisted, viewing the situation from this perspective provided a small measure of comfort. It was clear that we were in the capable and experienced hands of a qualified professional, even the more, Our Heavenly Father. ***He is always able*** and equipped to guide us through the most challenging trials, ensuring that we reach our ultimate destination and fulfill our destiny - in short, He is exceedingly qualified! It is peculiar, however, that we never ask to examine the qualifications of our pilots, doctors, and other professionals, yet we sometimes doubt the competence and credibility of God. This reminds me of the children of Israel's skepticism in Psalm 78:19, as they questioned whether God could provide them with sustenance in the wilderness.

They spoke against God; they said, "Can God really spread a table in the wilderness?

Psalms 78:19

In the event that we are ever inclined to question the ability and capacity of God, it is important that we do not lose hope or faith. The scriptures serve as a guide, providing protection and comfort during times of calamity. A verse that comes to mind is found in **Jude 1: 24-25:**

"Now unto him that is able to keep you from falling, and to present you faultless before the presence of his glory with exceeding joy, To the only wise God our Saviour, be glory and majesty, dominion and power, both now and ever."

The Message Bible provides a contemporary interpretation:

"And now to him who can keep you on your feet, standing tall in his bright presence, fresh and celebrating—to our one God, our only Savior, through Jesus Christ, our Master, be glory, majesty, strength, and rule before all time, and now, and to the end of all time."

Regardless of the version of the Bible you read, scripture provides us with the assurance that the God of our fathers, our Great High Priest, is not only capable but fully able to see us through and bring us to a perfected end. This truth has been demonstrated time and time again throughout the scriptures. When seeking mechanical work for my car or home repairs, I typically gather multiple references and speak with those who have worked with the individual or company in question. This allows me to gain a view or sense of the experiences others have had in working with them. This approach is particularly important in the business world.

Many businesses, particularly those in the hospitality industry such as hotels and rental car agencies, place a high value on our patronage due to the fact that we have the freedom to spend our money wherever we choose. Typically, these establishments will distribute surveys and questionnaires to gauge the quality of their service, our overall experience, and the likelihood of us returning or recommending their services to others. This feedback serves as a means of demonstrating their commitment to meeting our needs and exceeding expectations. Similarly, it is important to remember that God is more than capable of providing refuge and strength in times of trouble, as emphasized in *Psalm 46:1:*

God is our refuge and strength, a very present help in trouble.

The Bible does not make any promises about a life free from calamity or a life of ease once we have devoted ourselves to God. However, God has assured us of His presence during difficult times. I

In ***Matthew 28:20***, we read where Jesus promises his disciples, **"*Lo, I am with you even until the end of the age.*"** The trials and tests we face presently may not be the last ones we encounter. Times of uncertainty are expected amongst the children of God, and we must rely on God's presence even in those difficult situations.

In his writing, Harkins referenced a quote found on the walls of the Auschwitz Concentration Camp:

"I believe in the sun even when it is not shining. I believe in Love, even when I alone. I believe in God, even when He is silent."

Even in the midst of tragic circumstances, God is present, even when it may be difficult to see or perceive Him.

The Psalmist's writing serves as a powerful reminder that difficult times are inevitable, but God promises to be our refuge. Even when our world is shaken and buildings crumble, God remains steadfast and has pledged to be with us in the midst of tragedy. Though we may sometimes feel abandoned by God during trying circumstances, this is not the case. As the old church hymn goes **"God Leads His Dear Children Along,"** It was written by George Young after his home was burned to the ground. **"Some through the water, something through the flood, some through the fire, but all through the blood. Some through great sorrow, but God gives us a song in the night season and all the day long."**

This is the kind of God that we are serving, He is not only a God of miracles signs and wonders, but He is a God of compassion, care and love.

David reminds us in *Psalm 37:25, I have been young, and now am old; yet have I not seen the righteous forsaken, nor his seed begging for bread.*

In essence, David is conveying that throughout his lifetime, spanning from his youthful days to his advanced age, he has witnessed a plethora of events. However, he affirms that there is one thing he has never witnessed - the abandonment of the righteous or their descendants being reduced to begging. This statement epitomizes the care, provision, and protection of a father. Upon examining the Greek language, one would discover that the term used for father or daddy is ABBA, which translates to Source or Sustainer. David acknowledges and comprehends that our God, the God of Abraham, Isaac, and Jacob, is our Source and Sustainer. He is abundantly capable of guiding us through our darkest nights and most uncertain times.

The adage passed down by the elderly states, *"He may not come when we call Him, but He's always on time."* This implies that God is punctual and reliable, a God that can be trusted. During my harrowing experience on the flight from Dubai to Zurich, I had to constantly remind myself of this concept. My solace came from knowing that the pilot was fully capable of landing the airplane safely. At one point, I made the decision to avoid looking out the window because the scene outside was quite unsettling. I witnessed the wings shake, and the ground below with houses, buildings, and cars, but could not see the runway. However, I had to trust the pilot because of his extensive training, skill, and qualifications. Ultimately, the pilot was able to safely transport us to our intended destination.

In certain situations, it is necessary for us to shift our focus from the visible to the invisible and have faith in things that cannot be seen, such as God's grace, mercy, and ability to guide us through difficult times. A thought-provoking query arises as to whether we can trust God's heart even when we cannot comprehend His actions. David's words remind us that God is an ever-present source of aid in times of trouble. Trust is a potent term that denotes a strong belief in the dependability, truthfulness, capability, or potency of an individual or a thing. For instance, while boarding the aircraft, I had to place my trust not only in the pilot but also in the machine itself, and believe that both would perform as intended. This is the degree of assurance we have in humanity and its inventions.

In various industries, be it aviation, landscaping, automotive, or technology, including handheld devices like smartphones, tablets, and laptops, it is an undeniable fact that none of these products hit the market without undergoing rigorous testing. This is because the reputation of a person or a brand is on the line. Whether it is a household name such as Apple, Microsoft, Gucci, or Rolex, the value of a name cannot be underestimated. Manufacturers will take every measure to safeguard their brand identity.

It is even more so with our Father God; He protects His name at all costs. **Psalms 46:1** states, **God is our refuge and strength, a very present help in trouble.** This reminds me of the story of the three young Hebrew men who were thrown into a fiery furnace. Despite having done nothing wrong, except for vexing the King and disobeying his order, they were thrown into a furnace that was heated seven times hotter than usual. Yet, they were not afraid. As recorded in *Daniel 3:17-18*, they said, *"If it be so, our God whom we serve is able to deliver us from the burning fiery furnace, and He will deliver us out of thine hand, O king. But if not, be it known unto thee, O king, that we will not serve thy gods, nor worship the golden image which thou hast set up."*

The scripture highlights their unwavering faith and trust in the Almighty God, who is more than capable of seeing them through their trials and testing. The underlying lesson in this text is to recognize their unshakeable position of faith in God, which remained resolute during trying times. Moreover, the text prompts us to reflect on our own lessons learned during difficult times. It is crucial to remind ourselves that our faith must remain steadfast in the God of our forefathers, just as it was for the individuals mentioned in the passage.

In addition, we know that on certain occasions, God may not extricate us from our circumstances, but instead chooses to stand with us amidst them. This can be inferred from ***Daniel Chapter 3 verses 24-25,*** wherein Nebuchadnezzar, after witnessing the three young men being thrown into a fiery furnace, was amazed to see four individuals walking unharmed within it. One of them was described as having a resemblance to the Son of God.

Then Nebuchadnezzar the king was astonied, and rose up in haste, and spake, and said unto his counsellors, did not we cast three men bound into the midst of the fire? They answered and said unto the king, True, O king. He answered and said, Lo, I see four men loose, walking in the midst of the fire, and they have no hurt; and the form of the fourth is like the Son of God.

The lesson to be learned here is that sometimes God chooses not to remove us from a difficult situation, but rather joins us in it and demonstrates His power. Once He enters into the midst of our trials, the circumstances are altered and the temperature changes. Rather than cursing the darkness, we should embrace it, for we know that Jesus is the light that will guide us through. Furthermore, we can take solace in the fact that God can bring glory out of our misfortunes and trials. In the case of the King, he was able to witness the true and living God through persecution and subsequently issued a decree that anyone who worshipped any other god besides the God of the Hebrews would be cast into the fiery furnace.

Then Nebuchadnezzar spake, and said, Blessed be the God of Shadrach, Meshach, and Abednego, who hath sent his angel, and delivered his servants that trusted in Him, and have changed the king's word, and yielded their bodies, that they might not serve nor worship any god, except their own God.

Therefore, I make a decree, that every people, nation, and language, which speak anything amiss against the God of Shadrach, Meshach, and Abednego, shall be cut in pieces, and their houses shall be made a dunghill: because there is no other God that can deliver after this sort.

Daniel 3:28-29

Remember, whatever you may be going through at the moment, God is both able and CAPABLE of seeing you through. Allow God to receive glory from your trials and circumstances today. Let the world witness the manifestation of God within you.

Chapter Four

HIS INTEGRITY

In the previous chapter, we discussed the omnipotence of God, God's capabilities. We acknowledged that He has the power to guide us through our darkest moments. When I think of our God, the Creator of the universe, the great I Am that I Am, I find numerous words to describe Him. Some of these words are not necessarily theological but carry significant meaning, such as the word "Integrity." In this chapter, we will delve into God's integrity. According to Webster's dictionary, integrity is defined as "the quality of being honest and fair." When we consider our Lord and Savior, Jesus Christ, we must have unwavering faith that He is not only the Son of God, He is also honest and fair.

Numbers 23:19 confirms this belief:

God is not a man, that He should lie; neither the son of man, that He should repent: hath He said, and shall He not do it? or hath He spoken, and shall He not make it good?

This verse affirms that God is not restricted or subjected to human limitations, unlike we are. It is also important to reiterate that "He is not a man." Throughout my life, I have come across great men and women who are sincere, honest, competent, and well-meaning, both within and outside the body of Christ. However, all humans have limitations. We may be sincere, but we can be sincerely wrong. We may have the best intentions, but due to our human limitations, we may not be able to fulfill a promise or follow through on a specific matter or project. This is not the case with God. It is emphatically stated that "He is not a man," and therefore, He is not limited like humans. He does not face setbacks or regrets because He is not a man, He is God.

Psalm 50:12 states: *"If I were hungry, I would not tell you; for the world is Mine, and all its fullness."*

This passage highlights the omnipotence of God, who owns everything including the cattle on a thousand hills. It underscores the limitations of mankind in comparison to the Almighty.

When God speaks, His words are deliberate and true, leaving no room for ambiguity. During times of hardship and uncertainty, we must find solace in the fact that God transcends human limitations and remains steadfast in His promises. I reflected on the unwavering integrity of the pilot during that turbulent flight from Dubai to Zurich, Switzerland. This served as a reminder to me that the Almighty God has our best interests at heart; not only is He capable, but His very character is at stake. Let us draw inspiration from the following verses that reaffirm the steadfastness of His nature.

Deuteronomy 31:8: And the LORD, he it is that doth go before thee; he will be with thee, he will not fail thee, neither forsake thee: fear not, neither be dismayed.

Deuteronomy 31:6: Be strong and of a good courage, fear not, nor be afraid of them: for the

LORD thy God, he it is that doth go with thee; he will not fail thee, nor forsake thee.

Hebrews 13:5: Let your conversation be without covetousness; and be content with such things as ye have: for he hath said, I will never leave thee, nor forsake thee.

Isaiah 41:10-13: Fear thou not; for I am with thee: be not dismayed; for I am thy God: I will strengthen thee; yea, I will help thee; yea, I will uphold thee with the right hand of my righteousness.

1 Peter 5:7: Casting all your care upon Him; for He careth for you.

Matthew 28:20: Teaching them to observe all things whatsoever I have commanded you: and, lo, I am with you always, even unto the end of the world. Amen.

Philippians 4:6-7: Be careful for nothing; but in everything by prayer and supplication with thanksgiving let your requests be made known unto God.

Hebrews 13:6: So that we may boldly say, The Lord is my helper, and I will not fear what man shall do unto me.

Psalms 55:22: Cast thy burden upon the LORD, and he shall sustain thee: he shall never suffer the righteous to be moved.

Romans 8:28: And we know that all things work together for good to them that love God, to them who are the called according to his purpose.

2 Timothy 1:7: For God hath not given us the spirit of fear; but of power, and of love, and of a sound mind.

Hebrews 4:16: Let us therefore come boldly unto the throne of grace, that we may obtain mercy, and find grace to help in time of need.

1 Chronicles 28:20: And David said to Solomon his son, Be strong and of good courage, and do it: fear not, nor be dismayed: for the LORD God, even my God, will be with thee; he will not fail thee, nor forsake thee, until thou hast finished all the work for the service of the house of the LORD.

Upon reflection of these verses, I discover fortitude, bravery, and moral excellence. They serve as a reminder that the God of our forefathers is boundless and transcends human limitations. Although trust in men, whether they are fathers, leaders, or spiritual guides, remains important, mankind inherently possesses imperfections. Conversely, God is limitless and self-sufficient, which distinguishes Him as the one true God.

The names attributed to God not only capture the essence of His being, but also represent His functions:

El Shaddai (Lord God Almighty)

El Elyon (The Most High God)

Adonai (Lord, Master)

Yahweh (Lord, Jehovah)

Jehovah Nissi (The Lord My Banner)

Jehovah-Raah (The Lord My Shepherd)

Jehovah Rapha (The Lord That Heals)

Jehovah Shammah (The Lord Is There)

Jehovah Tsidkenu
(The Lord Our Righteousness)

Jehovah Mekoddishkem
(The Lord Who Sanctifies You)

El Olam (The Everlasting God)

Elohim (God)

Qanna (Jealous)
Jehovah Jireh (The Lord Will Provide)

Jehovah Shalom (The Lord Is Peace)

Jehovah Sabaoth (The Lord of Hosts)

Take a moment to carefully consider the list of names attributed to God. It is important to note that these names are just a few of the many that describe Him. Regardless of your situation, one of His attributes can be applied to help you.

In addition to God's integrity, we must also consider His character, which can be defined as a person's good reputation. For example, the pilot who was tasked with flying us to our intended destination had his character and qualifications thoroughly checked before being entrusted with the responsibility. When we think of the qualities that make up God's reputation, there can be no room for doubt.

I am reminded of Steve Harvey's hypothetical introduction of Jesus to the world. Here is what he said: *"Ladies and gentlemen, it is an honor for me to introduce a man who needs no introduction. His credits are too long to list, He has done the impossible time after time, He hails by way of a manger from Bethlehem through heaven, his mother is still headlining in the Catholic Church today. His DADDY is the author of a book which is the best seller since the beginning of time, He holds the record of the world's best fish fry. He fed five thousand souls besides women and children with two fish and five loaves of bread. He can walk on water, He can turn water into wine, with no special effects and no camera tricks. He has a head shot of every church across the country, even before the kings of comedy He was hailed the King of all kings, Ruler of the Universe, Alpha and Omega, Beginning and the End, The First and The Last, the Rose of Sharon, the Bright and Morning Star, the Lilly of the Valley, and the Prince of Peace. His name is Jesus, Jesus, Jesus the Son of the Living God."*

Upon my initial hearing, I was awestruck by the impressive resume of this individual. Clearly, it speaks to their exceptional character, integrity, and extensive accomplishments. The individual in question is none other than Jesus the Christ, the Son of the Living God.

In the book of **Matthew 16:13-18**, we read that as Jesus approached the coasts of Caesarea Philippi, He asked His disciples a question, **"Whom do men say that I the Son of man am?" Some responded that he was John the Baptist, while others believed he was Elijah or Jeremiah, or one of the prophets. Jesus then asked His disciples, "But whom say ye that I am?"**

In **Matthew 16:16**, Simon Peter declared to Jesus, **"Thou art the Christ, the Son of the living God."** Jesus responded by blessing Peter and stating that this revelation was not from flesh and blood, but from God the Father. Jesus then declared that Peter was the rock upon which he would build his church, and that not even the gates of hell would prevail against it. Additionally, Jesus promised to give Peter the keys to the kingdom of heaven, granting him the authority to bind and loose on earth and in heaven. Finally, Jesus instructed his disciples to keep his identity as the Christ a secret.

It is crucial for us to not only be familiar with the names of God but also to understand His character, abilities, capabilities, and integrity. This comprehensive knowledge enables us to confidently face uncertain circumstances and challenges, similar to how Job declared, ***"I know my redeemer lives, and He will come through for me."*** As children of God, we should unwaveringly trust in His integrity. The scriptures are filled with countless examples of God's immense power in the most unfavorable conditions. Here is a powerful song we used to sing regarding this subject:

I don't feel no ways tired; I have come too far from where I started from, nobody told me that the road would be easy, but I don't believe He brought me this far to leave me.

James Cleveland

Possessing unwavering confidence, in the most challenging situations is a must for us all. This was precisely what enabled me to maintain my composure during that tumultuous flight. I relied on the unshakeable integrity of God and His steadfast promises, reminding myself that He had pledged never to abandon or forsake me. As you read this book, I pray that you too will experience a renewal of confidence in God in your mind and spirit, finding solace in the knowledge that if you have accepted Jesus Christ as your Lord and Savior you are in God's perfect hands.

Jonah serves as a prime example of God's integrity and His compassion for humanity. Despite Jonah's initial disobedience to God's commands, he found himself rescued from the belly of a whale after fervently calling out to God. This is a testament to God's unwavering integrity and infinite compassion for humanity.

The notion of a god with limitations is unfathomable, and I am grateful that our God is boundless. As declared in scriptures, ***"He is able to do for us more exceedingly abundantly than we can ever think or ask for."*** We need not fret or question whether God can or will assist us since His honesty and character speak for themselves. This infinite quality of God reinforces His reliability and dependability.

Moreover, the lives of Job, Daniel, Shadrach, Meshach, and Abednego are powerful illustrations of faithful individuals who encountered daunting circumstances beyond their control and witnessed firsthand the profound integrity of God. Despite enduring the blazing furnace and lion's den, as well as confronting poverty and loss, they persisted in their unwavering trust in God's boundless power and had complete trust in His integrity. I am reminded of this song:

I must have the Savior with me, For I dare not go alone, I must feel His presence near me, And His arm around me thrown.

Then my soul shall fear no ill; Let Him lead me where He will, I will go without a murmur, And His footsteps follow still.

I must have the Savior with me, For my faith at best is weak; He can whisper words of comfort, That no other voice can speak.

I must have the Savior with me in the onward march of life, Through the tempest and the sunshine, Through the battle and the strife.

I must have the Savior with me, And His eye the way must guide, Till I reach the vale of Jordan, Till I gain the other side.

The Savior with me
Frances J Crosby

It is a source of comfort to be aware of the proximity of God's footsteps. I greatly value timeless hymns and songs; they have a calming effect on any situation. In difficult times when our faith is being tested, we must anchor our faith in the unwavering integrity of God. In my personal situation, I had to put my trust in the pilot's integrity, I had no other option. At an altitude of thirty thousand feet, I had no means of escape, and the plane would not come to a halt in mid-air to cater to my fears. I had no option but to trust the pilot and the airplane's integrity, even though we were going through a challenging few minutes that felt like eternity. This experience taught me a valuable lesson in how we ought to approach our relationship with our Heavenly Father. Even when we are faced with circumstances beyond our control, we must trust in Him unequivocally, recognizing that, unlike humans, He is not bound by any limitations. We must trust Him even during times of confusion and uncertainty, with the firm conviction that He always has our best interests at heart. The responsibility of the pilot and crew was to ensure a safe and successful journey to our destination, which they accomplished. Although transportation by plane or train may present potential risks, we continue to rely on these methods because of their convenience and efficiency.

Our Creator God has our best interests in mind and watches over us, guiding us towards our eternal destination even through storms or turbulence. We can trust in God to see us through any obstacle, He is the reliable and trustworthy God. His unwavering integrity assures us that He will not fail us, unlike the possibility of repeated failure with others.

Chapter Five

HE HAS PLANS FOR YOU

Upon boarding the aircraft in Dubai for my return journey to the United States via-Zurich, I had no expectation that my itinerary would be subject to potential disruption. Naturally, both the pilots and crew had the same goal in mind, which was to ensure the safe arrival of all passengers at our intended destination.

On numerous occasions, we embark on a journey or set out to accomplish a task only to encounter unexpected disruptions that are beyond our control. In such situations, it is common to experience a sense of panic or the fight or flight response. This was precisely the scenario that unfolded during my flight.

Jeremiah 29:11 states: ***"For I know the plans I have for you," declares the Lord, "plans to prosper you and not to harm you, plans to give you hope and a future."***

This passage provided me with a profound sense of tranquility and confidence, serving as a reminder that the situation I was experiencing was not in alignment with God's intended path for my life.

I am sure all of us at some point or another have thought about our future and the plans we have made. We even go as far as asking the pertinent questions, where would I like to be, this time next year, or in the next five years? We can try and plan for the future, but life can change in an instant. How do we know what the ending is going to be like?

We all have questions concerning the future, and rightfully so, similar to the doubts I had during the flight that appeared to be doomed at the time. However, we can have confidence that no matter what occurs, God has a great plan for us. He is a benevolent God, and we are redeemed by His sacrifice.

Jeremiah received a message affirming that God's plans for us are good and filled with hope. This statement reflects God's faithfulness and purpose towards us, giving us confidence that His plans are never evil even during times of uncertainty. Whether we are anticipating the future, planning for retirement, relocating or setting goals, we can trust that God has great plans for each of us, and we can have open and honest dialogue with God about these plans.

The question at hand is a simple yet profound one:

What is the plan, and why do I not know about it? If this plan is meant for me, it only makes sense that I should have some understanding of what it entails. After all, how can I prepare for any potential challenges or uncertainties if I am completely in the dark? It feels unfair to be left in such a state of uncertainty.

In many ways, this situation is like that of a pilot entering the cockpit of an airplane. Every successful flight begins with a plan, a roadmap to guide the pilot to their desired destination. And yet, when it comes to our own lives, all we seem to hear from God is, **"I know the plans."** This can be a disheartening thought if we lack trust and confidence in Him.

But perhaps there is a reason why God does not always share the details of His plans with us. Could it be that He is a sovereign God, omnipotent and omniscient at the same time? If we were given a complete picture of our lives, would we be able to handle it? Would we have the strength and courage to face the challenges that lie ahead?

It is worth considering that sometimes, the best thing we can do is simply trust in God's plan for our lives. Even if we do not have all the answers, we can have faith that He is guiding us in the right direction. After all, as the saying goes, ***"God's plan is always the best plan."***

The beauty of God lies in His ability to guide us through our journeys without divulging all the details. Consider Joseph's story - from being despised by his own brothers for a mere coat to being thrown into a pit, sold into slavery, and eventually imprisoned before reaching the palace, Joseph was never given the full picture. Had he known the extent of his trials beforehand, he too may have rejected God's plan. The challenges that Joseph faced were seemingly insurmountable, yet

God remained by his side every step of the way. In the end, Joseph was able to find solace in the fact that what was meant to harm him, God used for good.

The concept of God's plan and providence is often a topic of discussion among believers. It is natural to question whether our struggles and challenges are part of God's plan for us, or if it is a deviation from his intended path. We may wonder why we are not prospering or why we are facing poverty, sickness, or depression. However, it is important to understand that the providential plan of God is not explicitly mentioned in the Bible, but its essence can be found throughout scripture.

The term "providence" is derived from the words "pro" meaning "before" and "video" meaning "to see." Thus, providence can be defined as "to see before," which implies that God plans ahead and is not taken by surprise by any event that occurs in our lives. It means that God did not create the world and then abandon it to its fate, but rather, He continuously watches over His creation and plans accordingly.

We are to remind ourselves that our struggles, challenges, and hardships are not part of God's plan for our lives. We should not accept bad marriages, poverty, sickness, or depression as part of our destiny. Instead, we should rely on God's providential plan, which ensures that everything happens for a reason and that nothing occurs by chance.

As believers in Jesus Christ, we must firmly believe that God holds ultimate control over all things, which is why we engage in prayer. Our faith teaches us that God is all-seeing, all-knowing, and invested in our well-being, providing us with protection and fulfilling our needs at the right moment.

God's plan for us is rooted in love, as evidenced with the giving of His Son Jesus for the restoration of Humanity.

For God so loved the world, that He gave His only Son, that whoever believes in Him should not perish but have eternal life. John 3:16

Our lives are not subject to chance or fate, but rather there is a specific purpose that is meant for us. ***Romans 8:28*** states **that all things come together for good for those who love God and are called according to His purpose.**

In challenging times, we may feel lost, bitter, and confused, much like the Israelites did as they were led out in chains. However, we can turn to God to guide us and reveal what we should do next and how we should live our lives moving forward.

Let me reiterate the fact that God has a plan for each one of us, **God has a blueprint**. Although we may not be privy to the specifics, there is certainly a divine plan for our lives. It would be inconceivable for me to serve a God who did not have a predetermined course for my life. I am convinced that God has everything under control and has mapped out our lives accordingly. Your current situation is not a coincidence, but rather a result of a divine appointment. God's plan is for you to have faith in Him and to be a shining beacon in the place where He has placed you. He has promised to take care of you and never to forsake you. Therefore, do not be afraid of God's plan. It is a providential and loving plan that will ultimately lead to our perfection. While pilots may be highly skilled and experienced, they still rely on navigation systems or other guides to reach their destination. God does not need the assistance of anyone or anything, He is sovereign and all-powerful. The more we anchor ourselves in prayer, listening to God and obeying His instructions immediately, the more of the plans for our lives are revealed, even when God seems silent.

Upon successful landing at Zurich International Airport, we, the passengers, despite being shaken and fearful during the approach, mustered up the strength to give a resounding round of applause. Our fears proved unfounded, as everything went according to plan, and we breathed a collective sigh of relief. As we disembarked, the announcement of "Ladies and gentlemen, welcome to Zurich" resonated through the cabin. We trust in God's plan for our lives, even amidst trouble, challenges, and uncertainties.

If we remain faithful and true, we will eventually hear the words **"welcome home."** Let us always remember that God's plans for us are perfect.

9 798985 757576